Musical Instruments

Trumpet

By Nick Rebman

level 1
little blue readers

www.littlebluehousebooks.com

Little Blue House is distributed by North Star Editions:
sales@northstareditions.com | 888-417-0195

Produced for Little Blue House by Red Line Editorial.

Photographs ©: Shutterstock Images, cover, 4, 7, 8–9, 11, 13, 14–15, 16–17, 21, 23, 24 (top left), 24 (top right), 24 (bottom left), 24 (bottom right); PNW Production/Pexels, 19

Library of Congress Control Number: 2022910652

ISBN
978-1-64619-702-6 (hardcover)
978-1-64619-734-7 (paperback)
978-1-64619-795-8 (ebook pdf)
978-1-64619-766-8 (hosted ebook)

Printed in the United States of America
Mankato, MN
012023

About the Author

Nick Rebman is a writer and editor who lives in Minnesota. He enjoys reading, walking his dog, and playing rock songs on his drum set.

Table of Contents

Playing My Trumpet **5**

Glossary **24**

Index **24**

Playing My Trumpet

I play my trumpet.

I blow into it.

I play my trumpet.

It makes a sound.

I play my trumpet.

It has three valves.

valve

I play my trumpet.

I press a valve.

It changes the sound.

I play my trumpet.
My teacher helps me
get better.

teacher

I play my trumpet.

I practice every day.

I play my trumpet.

I read sheet music.

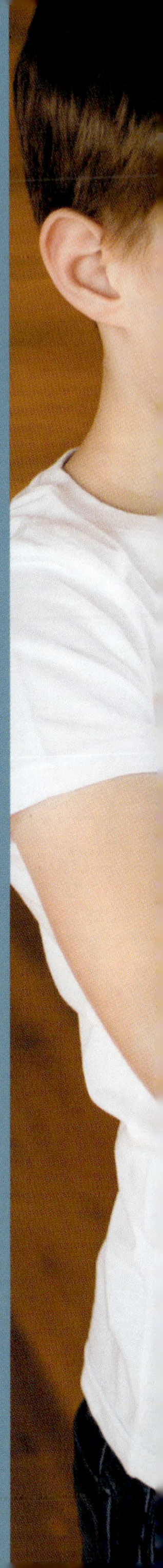

sheet music

I play my trumpet.

My sister listens to me.

sister

I play my trumpet.

I am in a band.

I play my trumpet.

We play a fun song.

Glossary

band

teacher

sheet music

valves

Index

B

band, 20

P

practice, 14

S

sound, 6, 10

V

valves, 8, 10